Kids On Earth

A Children's Documentary Series Exploring Global Culture & The Natural World

Norway

Sensei Paul David

COPYRIGHT PAGE

Kids On Earth - A Children's Documentary Series Exploring Global Cultures & The Natural World: Norway
by Sensei Paul David,

Copyright © 2023.

All rights reserved.

978-1-77848-280-9 KoE_Norway_Ingram_HardBook

978-1-77848-279-3 KoE_Norway_Ingram_PaperBook

978-1-77848-278-6 KoE_Norway_Amazon_PaperBook

978-1-77848-277-9 KoE_Norway_Amazon_eBook

This book is not authorized for free distribution copying.

www.senseipublishing.com

@senseipublishing
#senseipublishing

Get Our FREE Books Now!

kidsonearth.life

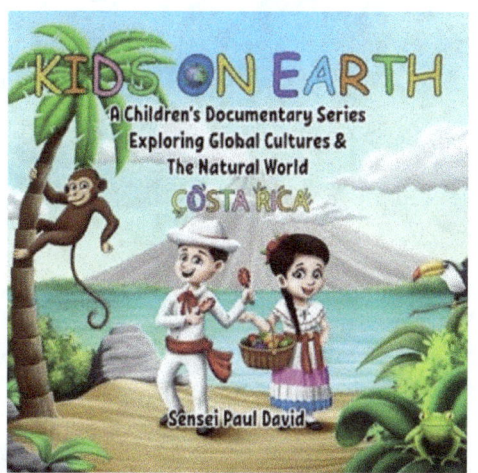

kidsonearth.senseipublishing.com

Click Below or Search Amazon for Another Book In Each Series

Join Our Publishing Journey!

If you would like to receive FUTURE FREE BOOKS and get to know us better, please click www.senseipublishing.com and join our newsletter by entering your email address in the pop-up box.

Follow Our Blog: senseipauldavid.ca

Follow/Like/Subscribe: Facebook, Instagram, YouTube: @senseipublishing

Scan the QR Code with your phone or tablet to follow us on social media:

Like / Subscribe / Follow

Norway makes up part of Northern Europe. It is nearly covered in mountains and has a long coastline where there are deep fjords and some 50 thousand islands.

Fjords (fyawdz) are sea inlets that lie between steep cliffs. It has some pretty steep mountains, and some are so big that no one has been able to climb them.

Are you able to find Norway on a Map?

FUN FACTS

Norway has a really long tunnel that is 15 miles or 24.5km long! The tunnel is called Laerdal Tunnel.

The capital of Norway is called Oslo and has been around for nearly 6 thousand years.

There are 2 sections to Oslo – a metropolitan area and an urban area. The population in the Metropolitan area is around 703 thousand people and the Urban Population is around 1 million people. That is a lot of people living in Oslo.

Do you know how many people live where you are?

FUN FACTS

Norway's official name is Kingdom of Norway or in Norwegian: Kongeriket Norge!

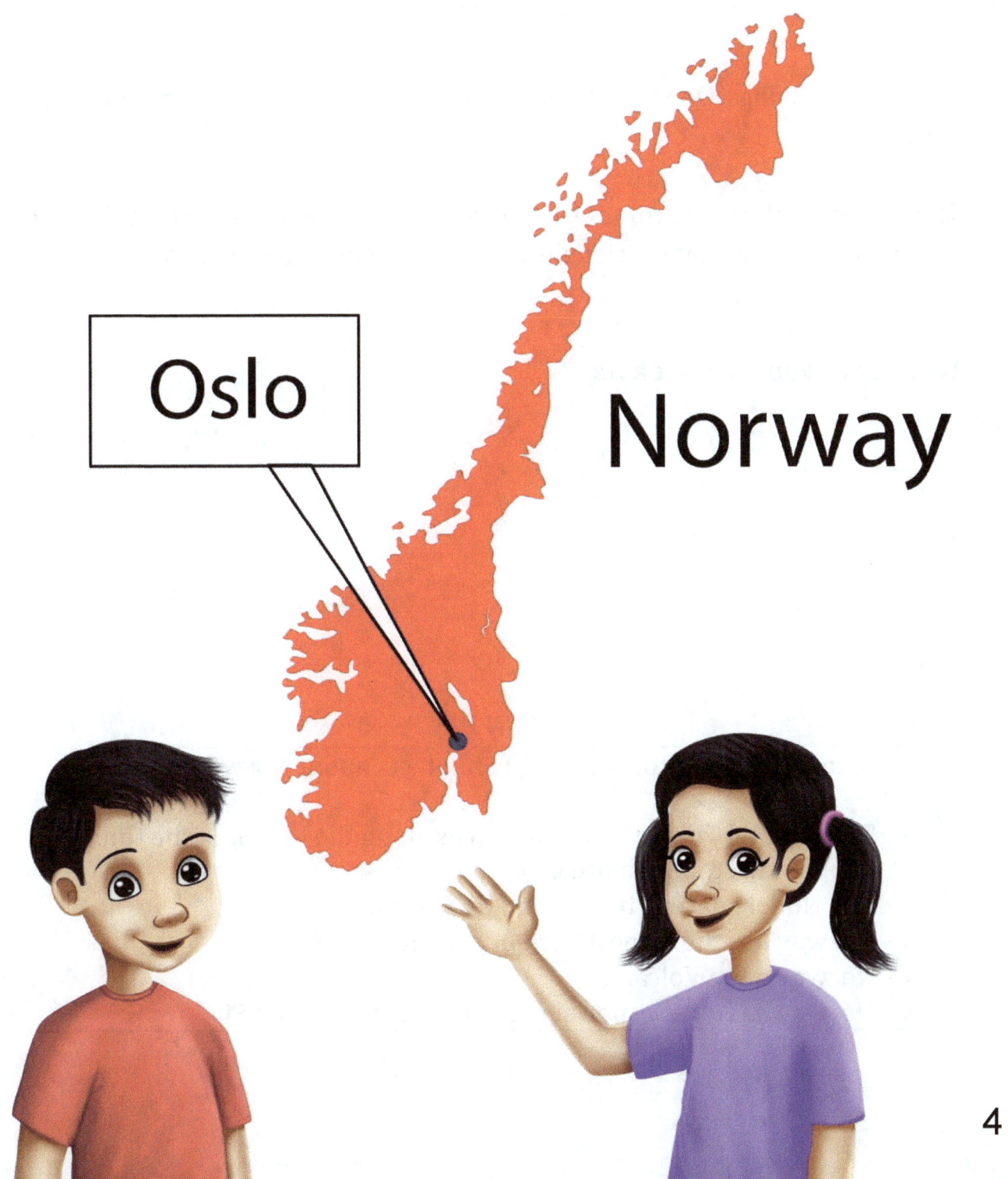

Norway has 2 flags. One for everyday use and one for when they have to go to war.

They are both the same colors – Red, White, and Blue, with the only difference being the War Flag have a triangle cut out of it, making it look like the flag has tails.

What does your flag look like?

FUN FACTS

Fredrik and I have put together a few fun facts about Norway for you.

- The Laerdal Tunnel has small caves along the length of the tunnel so people can stop for a break.
- The Nobel Peace Prize is given in Norway.
- Norway has the biggest herd of Wild Reindeer
- Norway has a Volcano
- Norway has a very special penguin who was made Sir.

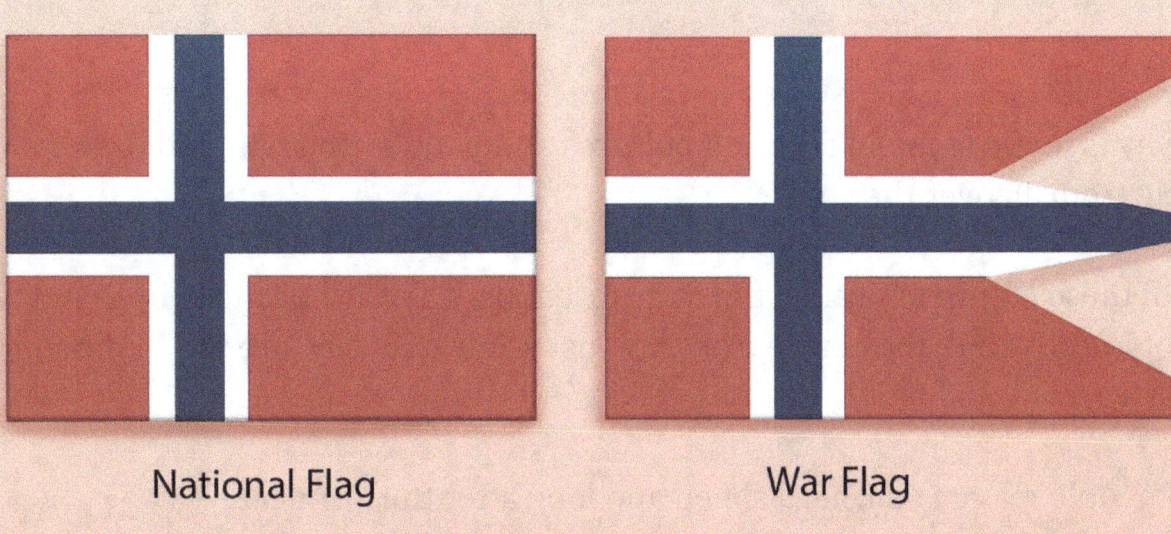

National Flag   War Flag

Norway is home to many different cultures and people. You will find in Norway people from all over the world.

One of these cultures is called the Sami or Lapps. They are Uralic people and we do not know where they came from, we just know that they are the first people of Norway.

Sami people mainly fish, herd sheep and look after the reindeer.

FUN FACTS

Uralic Language is made up of 38 different languages and is named after a mountain range called the Ural Mountains.

Can you ask your mum or dad to help you look up the Uralic Language and find all the different languages that are spoken?

Norway is a beautiful country and brings people from all over the world. One of the natural beauties that are in Norway is called the Aurora Borealis.

The Aurora Borealis is also called the Northern Lights and has very pretty colors. The colors come from the mixing of solar winds and the earth's atmospheric gases.

Can you name all the colors in the Aurora Borealis? Ask mum or dad to show you a picture or maybe a video of the Aurora Borealis?

FUN FACTS

You can see the Aurora Borealis from many different places around the world. But when you go to see them in Norway, you get the best view.

There are 2 different Auroras – The Aurora Borealis and the Aurora Australis.

Can you find the differences between the two?

Norway is connected to 3 different oceans and 3 different countries. These oceans are
- The Barents Sea towards the North
- The Norwegian Sea and the North Sea to the West and
- Skagerrak or the Skager Strait to the South.

Norway shares its borders to the east with
- Sweden
- Finland and
- Russia

FUN FACTS

A Viking was the first to be king of Norway. Vikings came from Scandinavia. Scandinavia refers to Denmark, Norway, and Sweden as a whole area.

Norway is home to some 2000 different plants. There are also thick forests where you will find 6 different types of trees. These are:

- Spruce trees
- Pine trees.
- Birch Trees
- Ash
- Rowan and
- Aspen

The ground is usually covered in moss and heather.

Can you find all those trees? What makes them look different?

FUN FACTS

The Spruce tree can grow to be really tall and is shaped like a Pyramid. It is often used to stop the cold winds found in Norway.

Norway has plenty of different animals that can live in the cold. These include
- Reindeer
- Wolverines and
- Lemmings

There are also other animals such as
- The Elk
- Red Deer
- Foxes
- Otters
- Marten
- Badgers and
- Beavers

Can you tell why some animals appear better off living in colder weather than others?

FUN FACTS

Norway's national animal is the Lion, and the national bird is the white-throated dipper. We also have a national horse, and that is a Fjord Horse.

Norway is made up of many different groups of people. We have the Nordic People that make up most of the population, there are also the Nord-Norge people, and the Sami.

Most Norwegians are related to people from Denmark and Sweden.

FUN FACTS

Greta and I have put together some fun facts about the people of Norway.
1. Norwegians are one of the Happiest People that you will find.
2. We love skiing and being outside.
3. The Norwegian language is spoken by 4.6 million people
4. We love to cook.
5. When we do not know you, we like to remain quiet.
6. We take our shoes off before going into someone else house
7. We love to read! Most Norwegian people read at least 1 book a year and
8. We love to drink coffee.

How many books do you read? What kind of books do you like to read?

Norway has 2 main languages. These are Bokmal Norwegian and Nynorsk. Bokmal means book language and Nynorsk means New Norwegian.

Bokmal is mainly used in school, and when communicating in commerce and communications. Whereas Nynorsk is spoken in the mountains and along the coastline.

FUN FACTS

There is no standard spoken Norwegian language. There are very small differences in how someone speaks, but it means the same all over Norway.

Norwegians can also understand Swedish and Danish when it is spoken.

There is no official religion in Norway. But all Norwegians do attend some form of religious gatherings, sometimes only for ceremonies. Some of the religions identified in Norway are:

- Evangelical Lutheran
- Church of Norway
- Pentecostals
- Roman Catholics
- Lutheran Free
- Jehovah's Witnesses
- Methodists and
- Baptists.

In more recent times there have been some Muslims and Buddhists as well.

What is your religion? Do you believe that there is a God?

FUN FACTS

Norway is a Secular Nation. This means that they rarely believe in anything other than what is in the world now. Many people think that is because money has provided what religion cannot.

The money of Norway is called the Krone. In English Krone means Crown. Norway doesn't use a lot of paper money or coins and prefers to pay for everything digitally.

We still use paper and coins, we have
- 5 different banknotes – 50kr, 100kr, 200kr, 500kr and 1,000kr and
- 4 coins – 1kr, 5kr, 10kr and 20kr.

What kind of money do you use?

FUN FACTS

You can use Norwegian money in Sweden and Finland.

In Norway, we rely on our Petrol Industry to help fund our country and government.

We also import a lot of different items such as food and things people use like motor cars.

What does your country rely on to help the Government pay for things?

FUN FACTS

Because Norway is such a small, populated country, we have one of the strongest economies in the world. Every year around 35 000 new businesses are started in Norway.

Norway has a Constitutional Monarchy. This means that the monarch or king or queen makes a joint decision with the government officials.

What kind of Government do you have where you live?

FUN FACTS

Norway has a special King Penguin that has been knighted. The penguin lives in Edinburgh Zoo in Scotland. Brigadier Sir Nils Olav the 3rd is the mascot and colonel-in-chief of the Norwegian King's Guard.

Norway has an interesting court system. Civil Cases must be taken to the local conciliation board, which is like a smaller court. After you have taken it to them you can then take it to the bigger court known as the Supreme Court.

How many courts do you have where you live? You might need mum or dad's help with this one.

FUN FACTS

Norway is a pretty safe country to visit and live in. But tourists sometimes have their pockets picked. Pocket Picking is when someone takes something out of your pockets, and you do not realize it until later.

In Norway, everyone is a part of the national health insurance system. That means that Norwegians have free medical care in hospitals, have some of their doctors' fees paid for, get free medicine, and the government gives them some money when they need to take time off work.

What type of health care system is available where you come from?

FUN FACTS

Norwegians are very loving people, and we are proud of our capacity to look after others. Norway takes in a lot of people from other countries that have lost their homes due to war or other reasons.

We go to school in Norway from the ages of 6 to 16.

Some of the subjects we study are Norwegian, Religion, Maths, Music, Science, and English.

We can learn other things too like art, other languages, and farm work.

FUN FACTS

In Norway, we start school a lot older than in other places, we start school when we turn 7!

Norway's inland population remained isolated from the rest of the world until around 1900. Because of this Norway has managed to keep a lot of the older folk culture. This means legends such as pixies and other magical beings are still believed in.

FUN FACTS

Today, around the world, our older culture is recognized as Norse Mythology.

In Norway when we hold festivals and celebrations, we usually wear folk costumes and do a lot of singing. A lot of our stories have trolls in them.

Some of our festivals and celebrations are:
- Constitution Day May 17. In Norwegian, it is called Grunnlovsdagen
- Midsummers Eve. In Norway we say Sankhansaften.
- St Olaf's Day. In Norway, we call this Olsok.
- Christmas. Norwegians say Jul for this holiday.

FUN FACTS

Christmas varies across regions, but one thing that we share is that we have 7 different cakes to eat on this day.

The Norwegian national costume is called the *bunad.*

Greta usually wears double-shuttle woven wool skirts or dresses which she then puts on a jacket with a scarf. Greta then adds something colorful, like a purse or her shoes.

When I wear the bunad, I wear a suit that is really colorful and heavily embroidered.

Norwegians have 2 bunaders, one for special occasions and one for everyday wear.

FUN FACTS

The Bunad came into existence during the 1700s. There is an institute in Norway that is dedicated to the history of the Bunad.

Maybe you and your mum or dad can look up the Institute on the internet? It has some beautiful pictures showing the Bunad.

There is so much space in Norway. This means that we are close to nature and love being outside and exploring.

In wintertime, we do a lot of skiing across the landscapes. We won a lot of medals at the Olympics because of our skiing and our long-distance running.

What kind of sport is your country known for?

FUN FACTS

Norwegian **Sondre Norheim** is said to be the father of modern skiing. During the 1800s he made his skis a lot stiffer so that he could swing and jump without being hurt. This design is what you see in skis today.

Hey Fredrik all this sports talk is making me hungry, and I am sure that the readers would love to hear about the yummy foods we have in Norway.

The Norwegian national food is Stew. It is made from Mutton and Cabbage. Mutton comes from sheep. We sometimes have Lamb Stew Parties!

We have a lot of sheep, cows, and goats that graze on our lands. We also have slow-growing vegetables and fruits and berries that grow around our land.

We eat 4 meals a day. Breakfast or Frokost, Lunch or Lunsi, Dinner or Middag, and then we have a late meal or supper which is called Kveldsmat.

FUN FACTS

Many of our meals in Norway feature 2 different meat, Fish and Reindeer.

Some dishes include:
- Gravlax – smoked salmon that has been cured.
- Fiskesuppe – a soup made of fish and vegetables, like a chowder.
- Brunost – translates literally to 'brown cheese' and is usually used on a sandwich.
- Fårikål – lamb and cabbage stew.
- Sursild – a type of pickled herring you can buy in supermarkets.
- Finnbiff – sautéed reindeer meat served as a stew.
- Smalahove – a boiled or steamed sheep's head. Not for daily eating!

Summer in Norway can get as warm as 25-30 degrees or 75-85 Fahrenheit.

But Summer can be short, and our winters long. We can get really cold, sometimes as low as – 35 degrees or -31 Fahrenheit, but we have gotten really cold at -50 degrees or -58 Fahrenheit.

How cold does it get where you live? Do you get snow?

FUN FACTS

Daylight varies greatly during the year. In Oslo, the sun sets at around 15:30 or 3:30 pm in December.

The native or indigenous people of Norway are called the Sami.

The Sami have their own language, as well as their own capital called Karasjok which has its own parliament. The Sami people live off of the land and work as reindeer herders.

FUN FACTS

The Sami are also skilled fishers and sheep herders. They also use all of the Reindeer when they catch it. They use the meat for food and leather and fur for clothing and shoes.

Earlier we talked about the Bunad and some of our celebrations. One of these was called Constitution Day.

Norwegians celebrate how they got to Constitution on May 17, 1814.

Many parades are put on by children, as well as general festivities.

FUN FACTS

National Symbols: moose (animal), heather (flower), and the coat of arms as shown above
National Colours: red, white, and blue
National Anthem: Ja, vi elsker dette landet (Yes, we love this country)

There are so many different landscapes in Norway.

There are Fjords and some of these are surrounded by snow-capped mountains and waterfalls.

There is a big lake in Norway called Lake Mjosa. It is long and thin. It is 62 miles long or 100 kilometers, and it is only between 1 & 9 miles or 1.6-14 kilometers wide.

There are around 50 000 islands off the coastline of Norway, and on some of these islands, you can see Polar Bears.

FUN FACTS

Although Lake Mjosa is thin and long, you will find a small island in the center! The island is called Helgoya.

In Norway, there are a lot of mountains. One of the biggest ones we have is called Galdhoppigen it is very high! It measures 2,469 meters or 8,100 feet high.

Hey readers, let's look up on the internet how to say that big mountain word. Fredrik and Greta have given you a fun way to say it, can you discover how it is said?

FUN FACTS

Norway has many mountains. Some of the peaks are so steep that no one has ever tried to climb them.

Have you ever seen our flag? Its colors are blue, red, and white.

The colors of the flag mean liberty and freedom. The cross is called the Nordic Cross.

This flag can be seen in other parts of the world such as Sweden, Finland, and Denmark.

Would you like a challenge? You might need an adult's hand to do this. Let us hop onto the computer or your phone and look up all the flags that look similar to Norway's! How many can you find?

FUN FACTS

The colors of our flag can also be found in another flag – France! The combination of colors is well known to mean freedom and unity between the countries that share the color. How cool!

In Norway, we only have really small families. All our relatives usually live in the same town or village.

It is very important to our parents that we become independent, meaning we do not have to rely on mum or dad for much. This means that we have to be responsible for everything we do.

We also have a strong belief that we are all equal. This means that everyone can do anything, and we use first names when talking to other people, including those older than us and our teachers.

FUN FACTS

When our families get together, we like to go on adventures. We usually spend our holidays down by the sea or in our very own cabins called hyttetur, and these cabins are up in the mountains.

Thank you for coming along and learning about our beautiful home, Norway!

Did you have fun learning with Fredrik and Greta?

Fredrik and Greta had a lot of fun showing you some of the different things that make Norway home. Fredrik and Greta are grateful for what they have here, and they like sharing their lives with other kids like you!

The Norwegian people have a humble spirit and work very hard, but they like it when others visit and learn about their country, the varied landscapes, the different animals and plants, and the different cultures that make up Norway.

When you learn about other people and places you appreciate them. All cultures are different and that's exciting so keep learning!

Thank you for appreciating Norway.

What have you learned?

Take this fun quiz to see how much you have remembered.

1. What do Norwegians like to eat?
    a. Pizza
    b. Fish
    c. Lamb Stew
    d. Chocolate

2. How big is Galdhoppigen Mountain?
    a. 4000kms or 2485 miles
    b. 2469 km or 8100 ft
    c. 246 kilometers or 152 miles
    d. 1050 kilometers or 652 miles

3. What are the native people of Norway called?
    a. Sumo
    b. Sami
    c. Sushi
    d. Salamanders

4. What is the national dress called?
    a. Dresses and Tuxedos
    b. Bunad
    c. Tunics and Pants
    d. Jeans and Jumpers

5. What is one of our sports called?
   a. Skiing
   b. Swimming
   c. Fishing
   d. Car Racing

6. What does the Norwegian Flag mean?
   a. Freedom, Unity, and Liberty
   b. Our Home Our Land Our People
   c. The Mountains are our Home
   d. May the cold never get to you.

7. What can you share with your friends that you have learned from this book?

Quiz Answers: 1C, 2B, 3B, 4B, 5A, 6A

Thank you for reading this book!

If you found this book helpful, I would be grateful if you would **post an honest review on Amazon** so this book can reach other supportive readers like you!

All you need to do is digitally flip to the back and leave your review. Or visit amazon.com/author/senseipauldavid click the correct book cover and click on the blue link next to the yellow stars that say, "customer reviews."

As always...

It's a great day to be alive!

Get/Share Our FREE All-Ages Mental Health Books Now!

kidsonearth.life

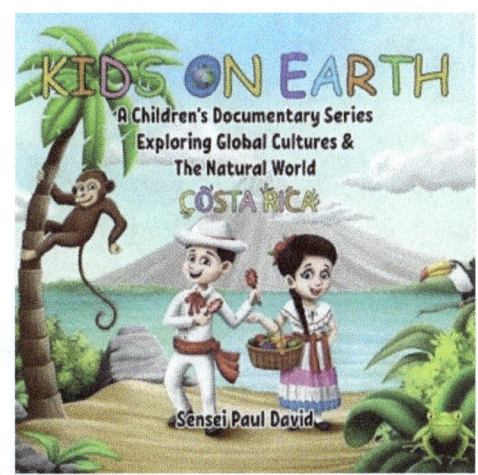

kidsonearth.senseipublishing.com

Click Below or Search Amazon for Another Book In Each Series Or Visit:

www.amazon.com/author/senseipauldavid

www.senseipublishing.com

@senseipublishing
#senseipublishing

Check out our **recommendations** for other books for adults & kids plus other great resources by visiting
www.senseipublishing.com/resources/

Join Our Publishing Journey!

If you would like to receive FREE BOOKS and special offers, please visit www.senseipublishing.com and join our newsletter by entering your email address in the pop-up box

Follow Our Engaging Blog NOW!
senseipauldavid.ca

Get Our FREE Books Today!

Click & Share the Links Below

FREE Kids Books
lifeofbailey.senseipublishing.com
kidsonearth.senseipublishing.com

FREE Self-Development Book

senseiselfdevelopment.senseipublishing.com

FREE BONUS!!!

Experience Over 25 FREE Engaging Guided Meditations!

Prized Skills & Practices for Adults & Kids. Help Restore Deep Sleep, Lower Stress, Improve Posture, Navigate Uncertainty & More.

Download the Free Insight Timer App and click the link below:

http://insig.ht/sensei_paul

About Sensei Publishing

Sensei Publishing commits itself to help people of all ages transform into better versions of themselves by providing high-quality and research-based self-development books with an emphasis on mental health and guided meditations. Sensei Publishing offers well-written e-books, audiobooks, paperbacks, and online courses that simplify complicated but practical topics in line with its mission to inspire people towards a positive transformation.

It's a great day to be alive!

About the Author

I create simple & transformative eBooks & Guided Meditations for Adults & Children proven to help navigate uncertainty, solve niche problems & bring families closer together.

I'm a former finance project manager, private pilot, jiu-jitsu instructor, musician & former University of Toronto Fitness Trainer. I prefer a science-based approach to focus on these & other areas in my life to stay humble & hungry to evolve. I hope you enjoy my work and I'd love to hear your feedback.

- It's a great day to be alive!
Sensei Paul David

Scan & Follow/Like/Subscribe: Facebook, Instagram, YouTube: @senseipublishing

Scan using your phone/iPad camera for Social Media

Visit us at www.senseipublishing.com and sign up for our newsletter to learn more about our exciting books and to experience our FREE Guided Meditations for Kids & Adults.

www.ingramcontent.com/pod-product-compliance
Lightning Source LLC
Chambersburg PA
CBHW081626100526
44590CB00021B/3619